HOW DO WE PREPARE FOR SEVERE WEATHER?

by Nancy Dickmann

PEBBLE
a capstone imprint

Pebble is published by Capstone,
1710 Roe Crest Drive, North Mankato, Minnesota 56003
www.capstonepub.com

Library of Congress Cataloging-in-Publication Data

Names: Dickmann, Nancy, author.
Title: How do we prepare for severe weather? / by Nancy Dickmann.
Description: North Mankato, Minnesota : Pebble, [2021] | Series: Discover meteorology | Includes bibliographical references and index. | Audience: Ages 6-8 | Audience: Grades K-1 | Summary: "A storm is coming! How do people prepare? What supplies and tools do we need to survive? Find out how people prepare for all kinds of severe weather. From tornadoes to hurricanes and blizzards to floods, we can be ready for anything" —Provided by publisher.
Identifiers: LCCN 2020045873 (print) | LCCN 2020045874 (ebook) | ISBN 9781977133496 (hardcover) | ISBN 9781977133434 (paperback) | ISBN 9781977154392 (pdf) | ISBN 9781977156068 (kindle edition)
Subjects: LCSH: Severe storms--Juvenile literature. | Emergency management—Juvenile literature.
Classification: LCC QC941.3 .D53 2021 (print) | LCC QC941.3 (ebook) | DDC 613.6/9—dc23 LC record available at https://lccn. loc.gov/2020045873 LC ebook record available at https://lccn.loc. gov/2020045874

Summary: Describes types of severe weather, how people can plan and prepare for severe weather, and what people do to rebuild after it.

Editorial Credits
Editor: Mandy Robbins; Designer: Heidi Thompson;
Media Researcher: Tracy Cummins; Production Specialist: Katy LaVigne

Photo Credits
Alamy: Sipa USA/Alamy Live News, 13; Getty Images: Mark Wilson, 19; iStockphoto: Deepak Sethi, 11, SDI Productions, 29; Newscom: REUTERS/Rick Wilking, 23; Shutterstock: Arthur Villator, 18, CGN089, 26, DeSerg, 15, FotoKina, cover, design element, 1, FrameStockFootages, 8, Hryshchyshen Serhii, 17, littlenySTOCK, 16, Makhnach_S, design element, Minerva Studio, 9, Nancy Beijersbergen, 5, Pat Lauzon, 6, Robert Blouin, 28, Roger Brown Photography, 14, Shane Wilson, 7, Steve Allen, 20, Suzanne Tucker, 4, Vadym Zaitsev, 25, wannapong, 21, wavebreakmedia, 27

TABLE OF CONTENTS

Words in **bold** are in the glossary.

WHAT IS SEVERE WEATHER?

A storm is coming! The weather will be rainy and windy. Weather describes the conditions in the air around us. Weather changes all the time. It can change slowly. Sometimes it changes very quickly.

A thunderstorm is one example of severe weather. It has strong winds and heavy rain. Severe weather can damage buildings. It can hurt people. It also harms plants and animals.

Types of Severe Weather

Weather usually follows patterns. Severe weather patterns are extreme. The temperature might be very high or low. There may be heavy snowstorms. These are called **blizzards**.

Heavy rain is another type of severe weather. It can lead to **flooding**. Rain often comes as part of a storm. Storms can bring high winds too. **Hurricanes** have very strong winds. So do **tornadoes**.

OTHER STORMS

Wind and rain are not a part of all storms. In a dust storm, huge clouds of dust blow across the land. Ice storms can coat everything in a layer of ice.

Predicting Severe Weather

People need to be ready for severe weather. A **forecast** can tell what the weather will be like. It warns if a storm is coming.

Meteorologists study **satellite** images of the weather. They might see a hurricane forming. Where will it go? A computer program will help them figure it out. Tornadoes are harder to **predict**. They can form with little warning.

A tornado touches down.

HAVING A PLAN

Severe weather can strike quickly. Having a plan is important. Companies, schools, and families all make plans for severe weather. Then everyone will know what to do.

Where do you live? Some kinds of severe weather may be more likely there. Different weather calls for different emergency plans.

An emergency plan will help people stay safe. It can tell people where to go. It will have a list of supplies they may need.

A family creates an emergency plan.

Practice and Drills

In weather **drills**, people practice what to do in a storm. Some schools have tornado drills. An alarm sounds. Students move quickly to a safe place. They learn what to do in a real tornado.

Some cities have sirens. They sound when severe weather is coming. There are warnings on radio and TV. Some people get text alerts. The texts say when to go to a safe place.

A teacher supervises a tornado drill in an elementary school.

Emergency Supplies

When severe weather happens,
stores may be closed. Many families
have an emergency kit. It is full of
supplies. It will be ready if they need it.

A good emergency kit has enough food for a few days. The food should not need to go in a refrigerator. The kit will have enough bottled water for everyone. It will also include a first aid kit. A radio is useful too.

A battery-operated radio lets you hear the news even if the power goes out.

Losing Power

Sometimes the power goes out in severe weather. There is no **electricity**. Lights will not work. TVs won't work either. This is called an **outage**. It might last for an hour. It could last for days or weeks.

Severe weather often causes trees to fall on power lines. This causes power outages.

A woman uses a flashlight to read to a child during a power outage.

People may have to go without electricity. An emergency kit should have a flashlight and batteries. A portable charger uses a battery too. It can charge a cell phone.

GET PREPARED!

Preparing for Hurricanes

Hurricanes have very strong winds. They cause a lot of damage. People listen to the forecast. They may be told to leave their homes before it hits. They will go to a safer area. They can return when the storm passes.

A storm wave crashes into a coastal road.

People can prepare their homes. They close **shutters** or put boards over windows. This keeps the glass from breaking. If it is safe to stay at home, stay inside. Stay far from windows.

Rescue workers save a family from a flooded area.

Preparing for Floods

Floods happen when water overflows onto the land. Heavy rain can cause floods. So can hurricanes. Sometimes flood waters rise slowly. Other times floods happen quickly. Floodwater can carry people and cars away. It can cover houses.

Many places have flood warnings. Sometimes the safest thing to do is leave. You can pack a bag and go to a safer place. It is best to leave before the flood hits. It is not safe to drive through floodwaters.

Floodwaters cover cars in a parking lot.

Preparing for Tornadoes

Tornadoes are funnels of wind. The wind is very strong. It can flip cars. It can blow roofs off buildings. It can destroy homes. Tornadoes strike quickly. People need to move fast.

There will be a warning when a tornado is likely. Get to a safe place. This could be a basement. It could also be a small room or closet with no windows. Use your arms to cover your head and neck.

A family gathers in an indoor bathroom during a tornado.

PREDICTING TORNADOES

Most tornadoes form in a thunderstorm. They are most likely to happen in spring and summer. Meteorologists track storms. They look for clouds that could form tornadoes. They send out warnings.

Preparing for Blizzards

A blizzard is a heavy snowstorm. It will be very cold. Icy winds can blow fast. Several feet of snow may fall. It is not safe to drive in a blizzard.

The power may go out. If a house uses electric heat, it may not work. It is important to keep warm. People gather supplies before a blizzard hits. They may be stuck inside for several days. They make sure to have blankets and warm clothes.

Preparing for a Heat Wave

Sometimes weather gets very hot and **humid**. It might last for several days. This is called a heat wave. Getting too hot can make people sick. Some people die. It's important to stay cool.

Closing the curtains is a good idea. Doing this can keep a building from getting too hot. People should also stay out of the sun. They should drink plenty of water. Find a place that has air conditioning. This could be a home, a library, or a shopping mall.

AFTER THE STORM

Severe weather doesn't last forever. But there may still be dangers right after it passes. Buildings may be damaged. Power lines might be down. It might not be safe to go out. Check with an adult first.

Homes may need repairs. People might need to refill their emergency supplies. We can all pitch in and help each other. If severe weather strikes again, we will be ready!

GLOSSARY

blizzard (BLIZ-erd)—a heavy snowstorm with strong wind; a blizzard can last several days

drill (DRIL)—to learn something by doing it over and over again

electricity (e-lek-TRI-si-tee)—a natural force used to make light and heat or to make machines work

flood (FLUHD)—to overflow with water beyond the normal limits

forecast (FOR-kast)—a report of future weather conditions

humid (HYOO-mid)—damp or moist

hurricane (HUR-uh-kane)—a strong, swirling wind and rainstorm that starts on the ocean

meteorologist (mee-tee-ur-AWL-uh-jist)—a person who studies and predicts the weather

outage (OUT-ij)—a period when there is no electricity available

predict (pri-DIKT)—to say what you think will happen in the future

satellite (SAT-uh-lite)—a spacecraft used to send signals and information from one place to another

shutter (SHUHT-ur)—a hinged panel that can be closed to cover a glass window

tornado (tor-NAY-do)—a violent spinning column of air that makes contact with the ground

READ MORE

Gray-Wilburn, Renée. *Hurricanes: Be Aware and Prepare.* North Mankato, MN: Capstone, 2015.

Hamalainen, Karina. *Extreme Weather and Rising Seas: Understanding Climate Change.* New York: Children's Press, 2020.

Schuetz, Kristin. *Severe Weather.* Minneapolis: Bellwether Media, 2016.

INTERNET SITES

Be a Ready Kid
ready.gov/kids/kids

National Weather Service Safety Tips
weather.gov/safety/

30 Freaky Facts About the Weather!
natgeokids.com/za/discover/geography/physical-geography/30-freaky-facts-about-weather/

INDEX